A FatCat Book

THE KING OF EASTER

Jesus Searches for All God's Children

Art by
Natasha Kennedy

Text by
Todd R. Hains

LEXHAM PRESS

BLESSED KING JESUS,

Thank you for coming to find and save the lost.
By your death and resurrection you give us
your life, your forgiveness, and your salvation.
Send your Holy Spirit into our hearts,
so that we may hear and
obey your word.

AMEN.

What is FatCat?

FatCat is our way of making the catechism approachable. He represents the catechism: the Ten Commandments, the Apostles' Creed, and the Lord's Prayer.

In this book, FatCat guides us through the truth we celebrate on the Holy Day of Easter. Our Lord and King Jesus seeks and saves the lost. He brings the lost out of death and darkness into life and light. He speaks his word and delivers them from destruction.

And today that is still true: in his word Jesus brings himself to us—his life, his salvation, and his forgiveness. From his birth to his death to his resurrection and beyond, Jesus seeks and saves the lost.

FatCat is hidden throughout the pages of this book. Search for him with your child as you enjoy this book together, and hide the truth of Jesus in your heart.

The man on the cross is the God who was born of a virgin. Wherever his name and word are, you will find him—with his life, salvation, and forgiveness for you.

Happy Easter to all God's children!

"The Sun of Righteousness will rise
with healing in his wings."
Malachi 4:2 NLT

Jesus is the King of Easter!
He finds who is lost.
Who is lost, he saves.

His mother Mary, who believed the angel's word—
did the King of Easter find and save her?

Yes!

Faithful Simeon and Anna, who waited for their Savior—
did the King of Easter find and save them?

Yes!

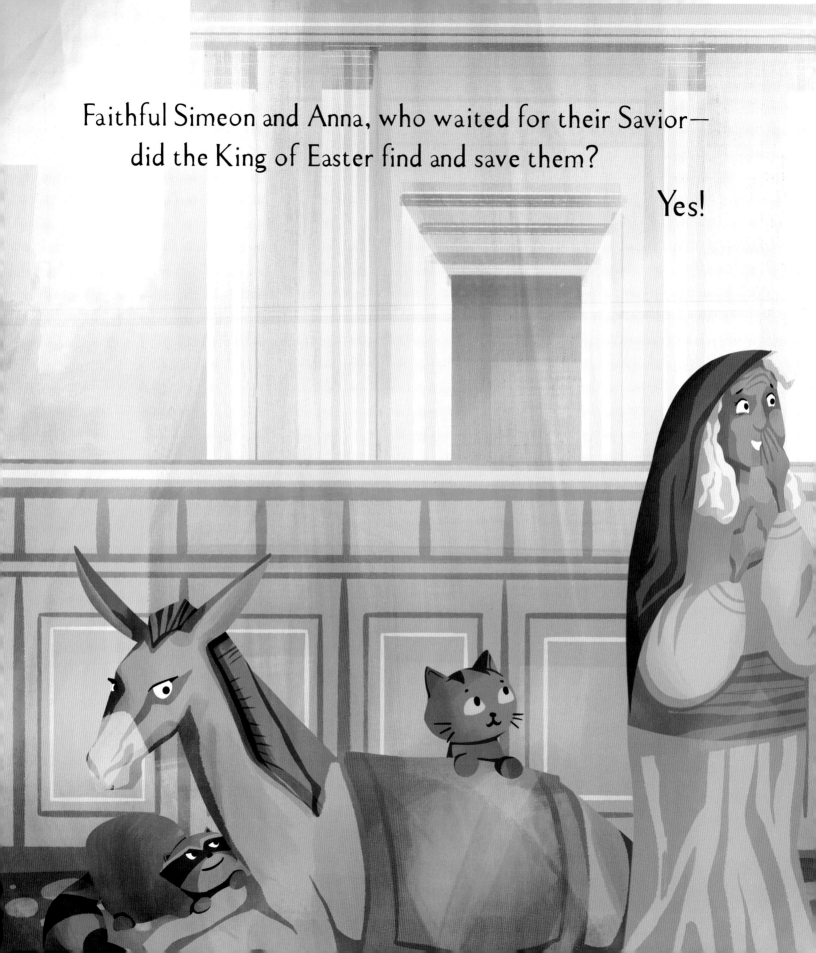

His cousin John, who prepared the way before him—
did the King of Easter find and save him?

Yes!

The tax collector Matthew, who was hated by his people—
did the King of Easter find and save him?

Yes!

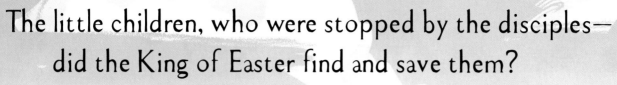

The little children, who were stopped by the disciples—
did the King of Easter find and save them?

Yes!

Small Zacchaeus, who climbed a tree just to see him—
did the King of Easter find and save him?

Yes!

His friend Lazarus, who died before he got there—
did the King of Easter find and save him?

Yes!

Martha's sister Mary, who was sorry for her sin—
did the King of Easter find and save her?

Yes!

The thief, who hung on a cross—
did the King of Easter find and save him?

Yes!

The centurion, who called Jesus God—
did the King of Easter find and save him?

Yes!

Today salvation has

come to this house.

Mary Magdalene, who searched for her Lord—
did the King of Easter find and save her?

Yes!

The Emmaus travelers, who had hoped for a Savior—
did the King of Easter find and save them?

Yes!

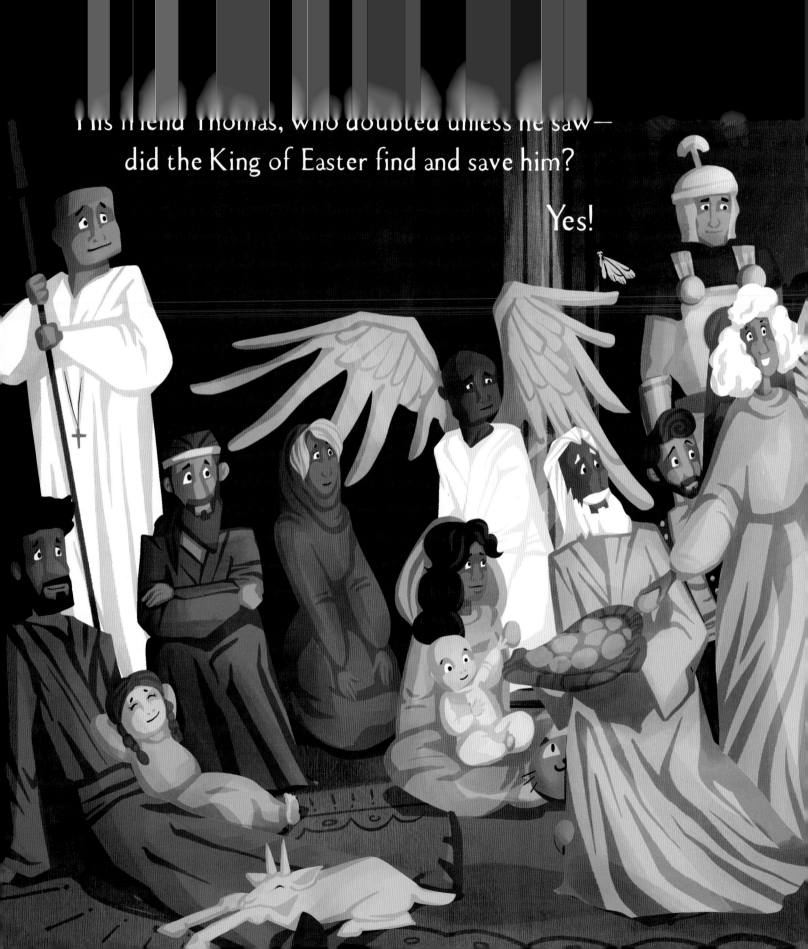

His friend Thomas, who doubted unless he saw—
did the King of Easter find and save him?

Yes!

His friend Peter, who denied him three times—
did the King of Easter find and save him?

Yes!

His enemy Saul, who found and killed Jesus' friends—
did the King of Easter find and save him?

Yes!

And you—
did the King of Easter find and save you?
Yes!

Jesus is the King of Easter.
He finds who is lost.
Who is lost, he saves.

Find Jesus and his friends!

Jesus

Genesis–Revelation
Psalms 1–150

FatCat

Psalm 145:14–17

Mary and Joseph

Luke 1:26–38

Anna and Simeon

Luke 2:21–35

John

Matthew 3:1–17;
Mark 1:1–11; Luke 3:1–22;
John 1:19–34

Matthew

Matthew 9:9–13

The little children

Matthew 19:13–15;
Mark 10:13–16; Luke 18:15–17

Bartimaeus

Matthew 20:29–34;
Mark 10:46–52;
Luke 18:35–43

Zacchaeus

Luke 19:1–10

Lazarus

John 11:1–44

Mary and Martha

Luke 7:36–50; Matthew 26:6–13;
Mark 14:3–9; John 12:1–8

The thief on the cross

Luke 23:39–43

The centurion at the cross

Matthew 27:54; Mark 15:39;
Luke 23:46–47

Adam and Eve

Genesis 3; Psalm 68;
Romans 5:14–18;
1 Corinthians 15:20–28

Angel

Luke 24:4–7; Matthew 28:2–7;
Mark 16:5–7

Mary Magdalene

John 20:11–20;
Matthew 28:1–10

The Emmaus travelers

Luke 24:13–34

Thomas

John 20:24–29

Peter

John 21:1–19

Saul

Acts 9:1–19; 22:4–11; 26:8–18

You

Isaiah 43:1; Ephesians 1:3–10;
Luke 19:9–10; John 17:3;
Psalm 121

Wormy

Knock Knock

FauxCat

Fudge

Psalm 145:14–17

Families are little churches.

We pray together. We bring our sin and sadness, our joy and faith to the Lord our God. We read the Bible together. We hear Jesus' promises for us. And we forgive each other, because God, in Christ, has forgiven us.

This brief service of family prayer is designed to be prayed responsively. The leader reads the plain text; everyone reads the bold text. Even though your children might not be readers yet, they'll learn these words as you repeat them again and again each day. You could use it in the morning or evening—or anytime you and your children read this book, even when it's not Easter time!

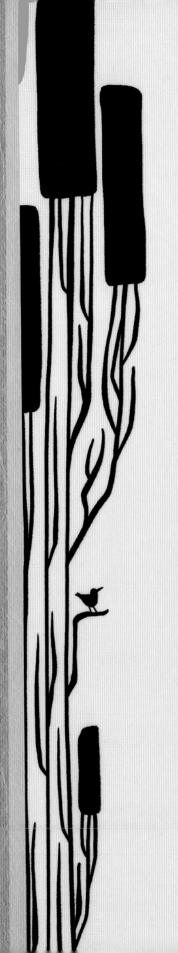

Easter Prayer

In the name of the Father
and of the Son and of the Holy Spirit.
Amen.

Christ is risen! Alleluia!
Why do you seek the living among the dead? Alleluia!

Luke 24:5

He sent his word and healed them! Alleluia!
And delivered them from destruction. Alleluia!

Psalm 107:20

I thank you that you have answered me. Alleluia!
And have become my salvation. Alleluia!

Psalm 118:21

Oh give thanks to the LORD, for he is good. Alleluia!
For his steadfast love endures forever! Alleluia!

Psalm 118:1

God has made us his people through our baptism into Christ. Living together in trust and hope, we confess our faith:

I believe in God, the Father almighty,
    maker of heaven and earth;
And in Jesus Christ, his only Son, our Lord;
    who was conceived by the Holy Spirit,
    born of the Virgin Mary,
    suffered under Pontius Pilate,
    was crucified, died, and was buried.
    He descended into hell.
    On the third day he rose again from the dead.
    He ascended into heaven,
    and is seated at the right hand of the Father.
    He will come again to judge
        the living and the dead.
I believe in the Holy Spirit,
    the holy catholic church,
    the communion of saints,
    the forgiveness of sins,
    the resurrection of the body,
    and the life everlasting.
Amen.

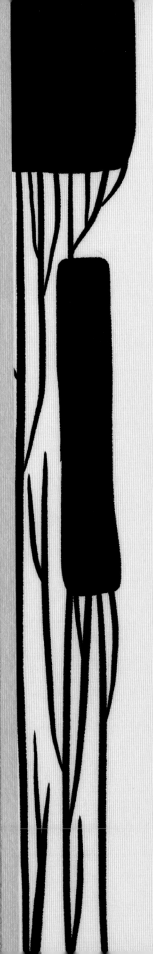

God is our loving Father.

He wants to hear our questions, fears, and joys.

Let us boldly offer our prayers for others
and for ourselves to God:

Parents, you might help your children pray
by asking questions like:

What are you thankful for?
What are you afraid of?
What do you want to tell God?

You might also pray the words of the Bible,
especially the Lord's Prayer, or the Apostles' Creed.
Make these words your own!

Blessed King Jesus,
thank you for coming to find and save the lost.
By your death and resurrection you give us
your life, your forgiveness, and your salvation.
Send your Holy Spirit into our hearts,
so that we may hear and obey your word.
Amen.

Let us bless the LORD.

Thanks be to God.

The grace of our Lord Jesus Christ
and the love of God and the communion
of the Holy Spirit be with us all.   2 Corinthians 13:14

Amen.

To Parents

Jesus came to find the lost and to save them. That's what Jesus promises Zacchaeus: "The Son of Man came to seek and save the lost" (Luke 19:10). The story of Zacchaeus is the story of all who are lost and found.

This book presents Jesus, the King of Easter, searching for the lost. "I will seek the lost, and I will bring back the strayed, and I will bind up the injured, and I will strengthen the weak" (Ezekiel 34:16).

Some of the lost don't seem very lost—the Virgin Mary and John the Baptist. Others seem too lost—the thief on the cross and Saul.

Some are searching for Jesus—Simeon, Zacchaeus, and Mary Magdalene. Others aren't looking for Jesus at all—Matthew the tax collector, the centurion at the cross, and the travelers on the road to Emmaus.

But they all are lost. "All we like sheep have gone astray" (Isaiah 53:6).

They all need Jesus. "He is our God, the God from whom salvation comes; God is the LORD, by whom we escape death" (Psalm 68:20 BCP).

When Jesus finds the lost, he brings them out of death and into life. He gives himself and all that he has to us.

And that's the story of Easter. On Easter Sunday, King Jesus rose from the grave, defeating sin, death, and the devil and bringing us forgiveness, life, and salvation.

"The people who walked in darkness have seen a great light; those who dwelt in a land of deep darkness, on them a light has shone" (Isaiah 9:2).

Easter celebrates Jesus putting death to death, bringing us out of darkness into light, and giving us true life.

God's word brings us Jesus, and Jesus brings us good news! Wherever his name and word are, you will find him—with his life, salvation, and forgiveness for you. As he promises Zacchaeus, "Today salvation has come to this house" (Luke 19:9).

The King of Easter: Jesus Searches for All God's Children
A FatCat Book

Copyright 2023 Natasha Kennedy / Lexham Press

Lexham Press, 1313 Commercial St., Bellingham, Washington 98225
LexhamPress.com

Printed in China.
ISBN 9781683596868
Library of Congress Control Number 2022940304

Lexham Editorial: Todd R. Hains, Veronica Hains, Lindsay John Kennedy,
    Mandi Newell, Abigail Stocker, Jessi Strong
Cover Design: Natasha Kennedy, Brittany Schrock

This book is typeset in FatCat.